EB

C000129009

Step by Step Guide on How to Make Money Selling on eBay

Matthew Scott

Table of Contents

Introduction

It doesn't take a brilliant businessperson to run a successful business on eBay. In fact, most of the success stories told throughout the years have been ordinary people that decided to take a risk. They were willing to put in the hard work while learning from their mistakes along the way. After thousands of success stories, the mysteries behind becoming a successful seller on eBay are no longer that mysterious.

EBay launched in 1995, and since then, they've continued to grow and be one of the dominating platforms for online sellers across the world. Their growth is not slowing down either. In 2017, they reported over 167 million users on their site. Of that number, 25 million are sellers, which means that a whopping 142 million buyers are active on eBay right now! Although eBay is an international company, 44% of their business comes from the United States alone, but there's no reason you can't sell internationally to attract that other 56% of buyers. Gross sales in 2015 were reported at $82 billion dollars!

I share these statistics with you to push home the point that eBay is an extremely viable option for those looking to break into ecommerce or expand their current ecommerce efforts. While many sellers choose to diversify between several selling platforms, the sheer number of customers and amount of money that flows through eBay means that it can operate as a stand-alone business for anyone willing to take the time to learn the ins and outs of product sourcing, eBay's system, and proper promotion techniques. It takes some hard work, but this avenue offers every-day people the opportunity to earn an income outside of a traditional job. Even if you it doesn't become your primary source of income, it can supplemental a day job extremely well.

As with any sales business, the core of being a great eBay seller is offering an excellent customer experience. However, even if you can offer excellent customer experience, there are a lot of other considerations. How do you find products? How do you list products? How do you expand your business once it reaches a point that's not realistic to handle on your own? Taking the time to study these details shows great initiative on your part, and it will ease the headache that learning from your mistakes will inevitably bring.

EBay isn't the only international company that allows people to buy and sell almost anything. However, what makes eBay different than most of the popular ecommerce solutions is the ability to list items in either "Buy It Now" or "Auction" formats.

"Buy It Now" listings function like any other ecommerce solutions. You list a product with a set price, and when people pursue your listing, they're given the option to buy it immediately. There is also the option to list products with a "Best Offer" feature, which allows people to counter your original asking price. You can either accept their offer, decline their offer, or counteroffer again up to three times total. This immediate sales function is popular for those that aren't willing to compete with others in auctions and don't mind the possibility of paying slightly more to ensure they get what they need. "Buy It Now" is perfect for common items, but it can also be used on rarities and specialty items where there's an obvious price point on the market or a "Best Offer" situation is ideal for the seller.

"Auctions" are sold to the highest bidder after a preset amount of time elapses. Auctions do not continue until bidding stops like you see in traditional auction settings. Setting up start and end dates on auctions can help affect the final sale price, as can promotion and the rarity of an item. In some instances, a bidding war between users may occur, which leads to inflated earnings. Auctions are ideal for rare items, uncommon lots, and bulk sales. In ecommerce, eBay is the best place to sell anything that is extremely hard to come by because it allows people to compete for the item, makes it easy to find, and most users that enjoy auction-style listings are looking for unusual items.

While some eBay sellers prefer to stick to Buy It Now listings only, the truth of the matter is that leveraging both styles of listing is going to bring better success unless you only sell common goods. There are options available, and it just depends on the products you are selling and your willingness to gamble.

Unlike creating your own online store that requires very targeted marketing, eBay allows sellers to sell a diverse range of products rather than focusing on a specific group of people or type of product. Remember earlier when we said that "the best customer experience" is the core behind a successful eBay business? That's because the better your reputation on eBay, the easier it becomes to seal the deal with sales. People rely heavily on the eBay feedback system to help them determine if a seller is legitimate or not, and eBay uses these reputation scores to offer better discounts on fees to sellers that regularly sell and receive positive feedback.

Considering the great opportunity here, if you choose to expand into other marketplaces, you'll already have a leg up on many aspects of ecommerce. It is easy to make an argument that eBay is the ideal starting point for the budding ecommerce entrepreneur. There's several reasons I make this claim:

- International market for sales all over the world. EBay is active in over 30 countries.
- EBay's extensive search engine optimization efforts make it easy for people to find your products through Google and other search engines. This includes Google's Product searches, which can lead to a lot of sales if you're using great keywords in your titles.
- Multiple selling formats, as discussed before.

- Discounted shipping rates help you save money.
- Discounted fees for good sellers.
- There's a huge amount of resources to learn from, including a large community.
- It's a safe and trusted website with over 20 years of success.

Are you ready to begin the journey? It will take some dedication and hard work, but there are clear paths to success on eBay. Will yours be the next eBay success story?

Chapter 1: What You Need To Get Started

Before you plunge into your eBay journey head first, let's discuss some of the things you'll require to get your eBay efforts off the ground.

Basic Writing Skills

You don't need to be Shakespeare, but being able to write coherently is a huge plus. The better your writing skills, the more professional your business will be and the easier it is to avoid any confusion that can result in returns or negative feedback. Some large eBay sellers pay others to write or edit their listings for them to net the best results, but at first, you should handle this process yourself since you won't have a huge amount of capital running through your eBay account.

Reliable Computer, Internet, and Printer

Having a reliable computer and connection to the internet is a must. The customer experience depends in part on your availability to respond to messages, make adjustments to listings, and review and take action when items are sold. While you don't need a fancy computer, one that constantly freezes is going to cause headaches and slow down your progress. In a pinch, even a cheap $200-300 laptop will get the job done. Some are able to operate mostly through their smart phone, but this will hinder your ability to print off labels at a reduced costs and do research quickly.

Time and Motivation

Without the motivation and time dedication required, any ecommerce or entrepreneurial pursuit is going to fall flat. If you are going to take the risk, you need to remain dedicated to your new business. For some, the initial time requirements may only be a few hours every day after work. As things scale up, so does the time involvement required from you. Automation and streamlining may become required as your success grows. In some cases, hiring help is a viable option.

Motivation can be difficult, especially when you already have a full-time job and just want to unwind after the workday is over. If you need help to keep yourself motivated, write out a list of the reasons you are starting a new online business. Put this somewhere you will see it often. Don't be afraid to dream big. Writing down goals, mantras, and motivators and regularly reminding yourself about them helps bring them to fruition. You can honestly do this.

Capital

The amount of money required to start an eBay business is far less than starting your own ecommerce website or a brick-and-mortar store, but you still need at least some capital to start with if there are any plans to scale up quickly. You will need to be able to purchase packaging materials, pay for shipping labels, and purchase products to sell.

If you have very little capital to start, don't fret. You can start with almost nothing. It may take longer to scale your business to a size worthy of quitting your day job, but it is possible. You can begin by selling items from around your house to raise more capital prior to purchasing products to continue your success. This money may very well have to all go back into your eBay business. Most of us have at least a few things we wouldn't mind selling. This also helps you become acclimated to selling on eBay prior to spending any significant amount of money.

An eBay Account

You'll need to sign up for an eBay account. We'll cover this in greater detail later. It may be wise to create a dedicated email address just for this purpose, especially if you plan on scaling your business. The account is free initially, but there are cost involved in the form of fees. Many listings can be posted at no cost to the seller, but using special options can incur some additional costs. After the sale of an item, there are additional fees based on the final value. This fee is typically 10% of the final price. This may seem steep, but other ecommerce solutions often charge as much or more. We'll describe this in greater detail in Chapter 3.

A PayPal Account

You'll also need to setup an account with PayPal. PayPal is a payment processing service that has its own "wallet" system for your money, but it can also be linked to credit cards, debit cards, and bank accounts for easy withdrawals. You really need to accept PayPal payments to sell through eBay, but having an account is free. The only catch is that there is a 3.5% fee on all Goods and Services transactions, which applies to all items sold on eBay. We'll discuss this more in Chapter 3 as well.

Camera

Having a fancy DSLR camera is helpful, but a decent smartphone camera can be suitable in the meantime. Taking the time to take detailed pictures is something you can't really avoid if you want great sales numbers. Not only does eBay require at least one image for every auction, but images are an excellent way to sell items and show customers exactly what to expect. When it's possible, setting up a dedicated area for your product photo shoots can help create more professional images and net more sales.

Products

This probably goes without saying, but actually having something to sell is the cornerstone of your business. There are many ways to procure products to sell on eBay. Typically speaking, you will physically have a product to sell. However, there are some opportunities to sell digital products and opportunities to sell products before you even purchase them (dropshipping). We'll discuss all of these topics in depth later in the book.

Shipping Supplies

It is smart to buy at least some of your shipping supplies before listing anything. This can include:

- Boxes
- Bubble mailers
- Shipping tape
- Printer ink
- Printer paper or printable adhesive shipping labels
- Bubble wrap and/or other cushioning

Having these things ahead of time is a good way to jump-start your positive feedback. If you can ship as soon as the next day, your ratings will go up quickly, customers will remain happy, and you'll get it off your desk so you can focus on something else.

Research and Knowledge

The last thing you need is knowledge through research. While learning as you go works well at the start, the more information you find from reputable sources, the better your chances of avoiding mistakes and instead making the best decisions become. Taking the time to learn about your business venture and what others have done before you can help you achieve success quicker and make your work smart instead of hard.

That's all you really need to get started. You probably have most of these things available to you already or at least they won't be hard to procure, but making sure to set yourself up for success from the start makes for a much easier transition from simply being an online consumer to an online supplier.

Chapter 2: Setting Up Your Accounts

While we have a little while to go before creating our first listing, it is wise to take the time to go ahead and setup your PayPal and eBay accounts so everything is familiar to you once you're active on eBay. We begin with PayPal because it is required and sometimes it can take a few days to handle verification processes.

Setting Up a PayPal Account

Step 1. Get Started

Go to PayPal.com and click "Sign Up" in the top, right-hand corner of the page. You can also set up a PayPal account through their smart phone apps.

Step 2. Choose an Account Type

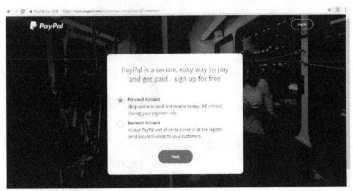

The next page is going to ask you what type of account you would prefer to setup. Note that you can use a personal or business account with your eBay account. A business account will come with some additional reporting tools, but all the fees are exactly the same. If you already have an account and want to change it to a business account, PayPal allows for this .For our purposes, we'll be setting up a business account.

Step 3. Choose Features for Payments

The next screen will ask you what type of payment service you want. This has three options: Pro, Standard, and Express.

Sign up for a business account to get paid

Pro service allows for some additional features that are only ideal if you manage your own ecommerce website, and it costs $30 per month. The Standard package is what we'll use because it allows for credit cards and all of the functions of eBay. Express removes credit cards acceptance, but there's no reason we would want to do that. So click "Select Standard" and move on to the next step.

Step 4. Enter Your Personal Information

The next page starts by asking for your email address. It may be wise to have an email address dedicated to your eBay business, that way your eBay emails aren't flooding your personal inbox too much. You just have to be sure to check on it regularly.

Sign up for a Business account

Enter the email address you'll use to sign up or log in

Enter your email address

Continue

You'll be asked to choose a password that fits their criteria (at least one number or symbol, and it must be 8 characters long).

The next page will ask for your name, business name, business address, phone number, etc. Once you approve and agree to all of the terms of service, you'll have to wade through a few more pages, but your account is essentially created.

Step 5. Enter Your Business Details

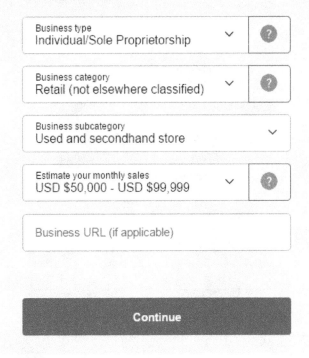

Tell us about your business

Business type
Individual/Sole Proprietorship

Business category
Retail (not elsewhere classified)

Business subcategory
Used and secondhand store

Estimate your monthly sales
USD $50,000 - USD $99,999

Business URL (if applicable)

Continue

Next, you'll be expected to provide some information about your business. Approximate your responses wherever you're unsure. This isn't incredibly important to have right other than the business type.

This information is required to verify your identity. This helps us to keep the PayPal community safe as well as meet government regulations.

SSN (last 4 digits)

Date of birth

The Patriot Act requires all financial institutions to ask for your Social Security number and confirm your identity to help prevent money laundering.

Enter your personal contact information

Home Street Address (No PO Box)

City

State
Select   ⌄

[ZipCode

Submit

After you press continue, it will bring you to a page asking for your personal details. While a first-time user of PayPal may be wary of this, you can use Google to verify that

PayPal is a legitimate and safe platform to handle your financial transactions through. Leaving this information out is not an option.

Step 6. Choose Payment Methods

The following page will ask how you prefer to start getting paid. For our purpose, we are going to click "On eBay" at the bottom of the list. On the follow page, it will link you to setup your eBay account. Right click this link and choose "Open in a New Tab." We'll come back to this soon.

In the meantime, click "Account Setup" above this link instead.

Step 7. Verify Email

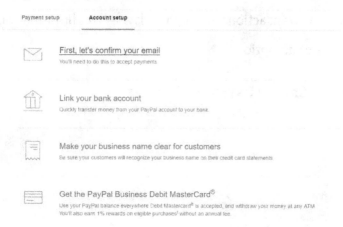

Click the link to confirm your email, and follow the simple steps PayPal gives you. PayPal will send you a link in your email that has a button that reads, "Confirm your email." Click this. Once you log into PayPal again, your email will be verified.

Step 8. Link Your Bank Account

Return to the "Account Setup" tab, and click on the link for linking up your bank account to PayPal.

This page will give you a list of banks, or allow you to enter the routing number for your bank on your own. You will also have to enter your bank account number. You can change this later if you change banks. Once your bank is linked, you are practically ready to use eBay!

Setup eBay Account

Now that you have a PayPal account setup, it is time to setup your eBay account. This process is fairly painless, and it can be broken down into simple steps for the first-timer. However, if you've signed up for an account for any website, you shouldn't have much to worry about.

Step 1. Go to eBay.com

Navigate your web browser to eBay.com. In the top left-hand corner should be a link to "register" right next to a "sign in" link. Click on "register" to begin the process.

Step 2. Choose "Personal" or "Business" Account.

On the following page is a form asking for your basic information. The first question is whether you'd prefer a personal or a business account. For our needs, we'll usually choose a business account. Choose a business account if the following is true:

- You intend to list items you've made or bought for the sole purpose of resell.

- You intend to sell large amounts of items on a regular basis.

- You use your eBay account to purchase items for your own business.

- You have a legal business and business name.

If you use a personal account, you'll still be able to start an eBay business without any major issues, and you can update your status later as things begin to grow. They work essentially the same either way.

Step 3. Input Names and Email

On the same form, you will enter your name or your business name. You will also offer them your phone number and your email. If you intend to run a large business on eBay, I suggest creating a separate email address for your eBay account. Otherwise, your personal emails will start to be overrun with emails from eBay that makes it difficult to keep organized. You just have to remember to check this frequently! I suggest using

Gmail.com for email services, as Google's reliability is difficult to beat.

Sign in   O Register

Personal account   • Business account

O Qualify for business selling limits, promotions, and get professional tools to help you grow.

Legal business name

Hi-Top Harry's Car Parts

Legal business email

hightopharry@gmail.com

Reenter email

hightopharry@gmail.com

Password

Show

Legal business phone

⁞⁞⁞ +1   (555) 555-5555|

We'll use this if you forget your password

When you Register, you agree to our User Agreement and acknowledge reading our User Privacy Notice.

Register

Step 4. Choose a Username

Next, you'll be asked to choose a username. This username will appear on all your listings, creates a URL for your profile, and is an important decision for a number of reasons. Most importantly, it represents your professionalism and business. Would you rather buy from someone with the username "Harry_666_4life" or "HighTopHarry?" It's pretty simple. Just use your business name or something close to it.

Step 5. Business Details

Next, enter your address or your business address and information. This is fairly straightforward and shouldn't require any special knowledge. It is important that this information is accurate because they are going to call or text you to gain verification.

Tell us about your business

Please enter your **legally registered** business address ana phone number. This is for verification purposes only.

Country / Region

United States

Legal business address 1

Legal business address 2

City

71P corl

State

Legal business phone

.S _ +1

Tell us how to contact you

We'll use this info to notify you about account activity, or nvthinn PIP th;:at rPnt1irPvnt1r ;:attpntinn

Step 6. Verification

Next, you'll have to *verify* your identity through call or text.

rfnV2?reqinput =43712a61799d8bd2ce38f891d56e4937b03fc42e4a8aa8289<

Verify your phone number

To confirm your phone number, we'll send a PIN to

.a **+11111111111** Edit

When you press Get a text or Get a call, you're confirming that you're authorized to add this number, and consent to receiving an automated text or recorded message in order to register. Text message and data rates may apply.

Get a text

Get a call

Questions?

Either method will give you a PIN number you need to enter in order to finalize your setup. After you receive the call or text, simply type in the PIN code.

Step 7. Choose Business Type

Next, we'll choose our business type. For many of us, this may be "sole proprietor," at least at this stage in our eBay careers. It will ask you to verify your legal address, name, last four digits of your social security number, and your birthday. It will ask for the estimate of your inventory value as well. This can be a wild guess if you have no idea. It doesn't impact anything important.

Step 8. Select Payment Method

Next, you can setup your payment method. I suggest using PayPal as your payment method, and then linking your PayPal to a credit card or bank account if you want to use that instead. This is the safest way to avoid the potential for people to gain access to your personal and sensitive financial information.

When you choose PayPal, it will have you log into your PayPal account to confirm this change.

That's all there is to it! You're ready to use eBay now.

Tell us more about your business

You're almost done! Please select your
legally reqistered busi ness type

reqinput =Se8b1400e01e5117a8b166a0a1b6c82cc87bb15fe44b5dc

Tell us more about your business

You're almost done! Please select your
legally registered busi ness type

Sole proprietorship

Harry   Hightop

5555

Please verify your personal address

555 55 St.

Chapter 3: The Cost of eBay

As with most major platforms for selling your products online, eBay isn't exactly free. There are several fees associated with each product sold. Having a general understanding of these fees is extremely helpful in determining if a product is worth selling, how much you can expect to make, and what is a fair price to list it at that gives the customer decent value but still nets a profit.

As a general rule of thumb, consider your fees roughly 15% of the product's selling price, including the price of shipping. This isn't wholly accurate, but within these parameters, you'll know that you are making a profit or if the item isn't worth selling.

To further break down how fees work with eBay, let's discuss their general fees.

Listing Fees

All accounts will receive at least some free listings every month. This is determined by your account status and how well you manage your business. It can also be determined by owning an eBay store, which we'll discuss at some length in a later chapter.

A standard eBay account receives 50 free listings per month. As this becomes too little for you, opening an eBay store just for the additional free listings may be worth it to you, but you have to weigh the costs and benefits for your own business model.

Listing fees may vary per category, but the standard insertion fee is $0.30 cents per listing over your allotted free listings. With auctions, you receive the fee back as a credit if it sells. This fee is permanent with fixed priced "Buy It Now" listings. Guitars and basses are always allowed to be listed for free (don't ask us why, because we don't know).

Final Value Fees

The final value fees are where eBay makes its share of your profits. This is typically going to be 10% of the final value that your item sold for, and for some reason, it includes the shipping cost you charged. So if you sell an item for $100 with $20 shipping, eBay receives $12 from this just for facilitating the sale.

The final value fee for guitars and basses category is only 3.5%! So if you're in the business of selling instruments, that's going to be a huge money saver for you.

PayPal Fees

PayPal charges a fixed fee of 3.5% of all money collected. If you receive $100, you'll pay them $3.50 to facilitate the exchange of funds. The only exception is "Friends and Family" gift payments, but these are not possible through eBay.

Putting These Together

Understanding how these fees add up has a huge impact on your ability to price your items fairly and price them high enough to generate a profit. Taking these fees into consideration, let's take a look at how making profit works on eBay.

Let's say we purchased a vintage vinyl record by the Beatles for $10 at a yard sale. What a steal! We check eBay, and the last three in the same condition sold for $90. That means we will be able to sell the item for $80 more than we bought it for, but that isn't the amount we'll actually make if we use eBay to facilitate the sale.

If we sell our record for $90 with $5 shipping, then we'll be expected to pay 10% in final value fees after payment. That means $9.5 in final value fee ($9 for the item, $0.50 for the shipping), leaving us with $84.50 total.

We also have to ship the item, which will cost us roughly $4 for postage and likely $0.50 for materials (assuming we bought in bulk). We're down to $80 that we'll receive after everything is paid.

If we had more than 50 listings created this month, we will be forced to pay $0.30 cents to list the item as well. This means we have $79.70 left.

Next, we have to pay the PayPal fee of 3.5%, but remember this fee is based on the total amount of money collected. That means 3.5% of $95, which is $3.33.

If we subtract $3.15 from $79.70, we're left with $76.37.

Of course, we also paid $10 for the item, which subtracted from $76.37 means we made a profit of $66.27. That's more than a 600% return on investment from the $10 we paid for this rare find at a flea market.

If this were a $50 item we paid $25 for, our profits would be much less even though at first glance it looks like we can sell it for twice as much of the purchase price. This is why it is ideal to always purchase products that you believe will sell for at least three times the amount you've purchased it at. This ensures that there is meat on the bones that justifies the time and energy involved in listing the item and taking pictures.

The Fee Calculator

I explain the fees at length because I think it's important to push home that profit isn't as simple as the value of the item minus the cost you pay for it. That said, the easiest way to calculate the fees to help determine if an item is worth purchasing is to use eBay's Fee Calculator.

Find this at: http://www.fees.ebay.com/feeweb/feecalculator

Fee calculator

Enter your information below and click **Calculate fees** to get an estimate of total fees for your item.

1 Select a category

Fees vary, depending on the category. For the most accurate fee estimate, please select all applicable subcategories.

Select category ▾

2 Select listing information

Listing details

Selling format	Starting price	Sale price
Auction-style ▾	$	$

Listing upgrades

This page allows you to type in the details of how you intend to list a product. We'll discuss all of these aspects in the chapter on listing your products, but suffice to say these options will have effects on the fee, as we described earlier. Using our earlier example of a vinyl record for $95 shipped, we'll see the following results after putting in our details and clicking "Calculate Fees"

Keep in mind that the fee calculator doesn't always consider that you may not have any free listings available still. Additionally, keep in mind that it doesn't include anything about the PayPal fee. You will want to figure in that 3.5% fee even after using this tool.

Reduced Fees for Top Rated Sellers

Once upon a time, eBay had what was called a Power Seller, and this used to be proudly presented on listings near the username of the seller and offer several perks. They've done away with this distinction and created Top Rated Sellers instead, but it operates in a very similar manner.

Benefits

There are a couple benefits of having Top Rated status:

1. Top Rated Seller emblem by your username. This shows buyers that you are a reputable seller. While it may not increase sales significantly, it can sway a few reluctant buyers that only work with excellent sellers.

2. 10% discount on final value fees. So if you normally pay $9.50 in final value fees, you'll only have to pay $8.55 if you're a Top Rated Seller. This sounds small, but this can add up very quickly and make a huge difference if you're selling in large volumes.

Requirements

To become a Top Rated Seller, you must meet a strict set of requirements both with your seller account and in the way you list your products.

For your seller status, you need to meet these few criteria.

1. You must have over 100 transactions within a 12-month period. This means 100 sales. In a pinch, you can try selling very cheap items that net you only a tiny profit to help keep this figure up while you wait for higher-dollar items to finally sell.

2. You must make at least $1,000 in sales in the same 12-month period. This should be fairly easy if you're selling items at $10 or higher, which is still a very low price.

3. You must upload tracking information when purchasing shipping for your sold items. This needs to be true for at least 95% of your sold listings for the last 3 months.

4. You must offer one-day processing and shipping on your listings.

5. You must offer returns up to 30 days on your listings.

If you meet the first three requirements, you will qualify as a Top Rated Seller. Fulfilling the requirements on shipping and returns will allow for the reduced fee rates. Do not stray from meeting all of these criteria. It's not only good for the discounted rate, but honestly, this stuff is good for creating a solid business with a great reputation anyway.

Taking fees into account prior to purchasing products to sell is going to make a world of difference in your profit-making abilities. It is paramount that you never forget about these fees. Because eBay charges their fees at the end of the month, it is important to make sure you don't spend all of your money prior to paying for your monthly fees.

Are They Worth It?

The fees on eBay may be steep to some sellers. Whether they are truly worth it or not depends on your business model and ability to buy low and sell high. For those that are on the fence, let's consider a few quick points:

- A brick-and-mortar operation has far higher overhead costs than paying for eBay fees. Additionally, the foot traffic cannot beat the online traffic that eBay receives, especially for easy-to-sell items.

- EBay has customers now. While you might be able to create a standalone ecommerce store and be wildly successful, promotion isn't everyone's strong point. You might prefer the eBay method as it comes with built-in customers, especially if you are selling popular items.

- Reduced shipping costs. It's true that other ecommerce solutions may also offer discounted shipping, but eBay's reduced shipping costs does help to offset the fees a bit.

- No special skills are required. Unlike starting your own website or opening a brick-and-mortar store, eBay is so user friendly that even those of us with absolutely no knowledge of computers can get the hang of it after a couple of months of use. Shopify's system might be the only full ecommerce system that can compete, but it doesn't have a built-in customer base. Amazon is appropriate, but it doesn't work well for all types of products and getting the most profits from them.

- Sometimes items sell for more on eBay. It sounds silly, but the truth is that some items sell higher on eBay than on Amazon. The reverse is also true. This can also be said about products in brick-and-mortar stores that can't reach the right audience as well; sometimes they sell for more online. (See the information on retail arbitrage in the next chapter.)

- Auctions of rare items are going to sell better on eBay than most other platforms. And honestly, the percentage an auction house would take instead may be far higher anyway. The same can be said about consignment stores that usually take 30-60% of the profit for selling your item.

- You can sell on other platforms as well. There's no need to stick only to eBay. So while the fees may be high, if you're selling items in bulk and need or want to move more product, then having eBay in your arsenal is a smart way to make sure you're not sitting on a large inventory that isn't selling quickly enough with only one platform.

- There are reduced fees for people that do a great job selling and handling customer service, thanks to the Top Rated Seller program.

Ultimately, if you believe you can open your own online store, drive traffic to it, and reap better profits than you can paying eBay fees, you should by all means pursue that avenue. There is absolutely no reason you MUST use eBay to be successful with ecommerce, and definitely no reason you have to use only one platform. EBay is a very useful tool, though, and it shouldn't be taken lightly, but you have options.

Chapter 4: Sourcing Products

An important part of earning a living through eBay is knowing where to find products to sell. The key is finding products at prices that allow for making a healthy profit. For many sellers, this ends up being a large part of their workload. There are several sources for products, including:

- Your own stuff
- Thrift stores
- Yard Sales
- Flea Markets
- Retail arbitrage
- Wholesale

We will take the time to explain all of these methods, but first let's discuss value and purchasing prices. While sourcing products, a good rule of thumb is purchasing products at a price low enough to sell them for three times the amount you paid. This rule works well because of the costs involved, which includes fees, shipping supplies, and other concerns. Buying products with a smaller return on investment may not be worth the effort involved unless you're able to move them in bulk.

Determining the value can be done using eBay sold listings. Search for your desired product on eBay, and in the refinements, choose "Sold Items Only." Find the last few items that best match what you have to offer, and you'll be able to determine the highest possible price you can afford for the item. Sometimes for items that aren't widely available through eBay, it is wise to take a look at the current listings as well. Knowing the current competition makes it easier to price.

If you're unsure if an item will sell well, consider the frequency of dates on sold listings. If an item hasn't sold in months even though there's still several listed, it may not be a viable sales item. Likewise, if the item sells consistently, it is definitely worth buying and reselling for some quick gains.

Now that you have a general idea on how to price and what prices you can purchase items at, let's discuss the many methods of sourcing products.

Your Stuff

It is my suggestion to start by selling your own unwanted items. Go around your house and make a pile of all the items you no longer want or need. This can be books, DVDs, records and CDs, video games, electronics, musical instruments, and just about everything else you can think of. Using the method we described before will give you a good idea of how much you stand to earn.

This is a great starting point for a couple reasons. Not only does it help to declutter your home, but it's the perfect place to start getting your feet wet with eBay without the worry of a large loss of capital. This method isn't remotely sustainable in the long run, but the learning experience and the little bit of extra capital you receive will help you start your business in earnest.

Retail Arbitrage

Retail arbitrage is the process of purchasing items in retail stores to sell at retail yourself, usually online. When products are priced well, there's actually quite a bit of profit in this method.

When you're shopping at a retail location, always make sure to venture off into the clearance section to check prices against eBay. Check prices against eBay sold listings, and if it meets the rule of thumb where the product can be sold for three times the amount it costs you, then it's likely worth grabbing as many of them as you can.

Thrift Stores

Thrift stores can be gold mines for used products worth selling. There's everything from CDs, DVDs, records, video games and consoles, and almost everything under the sun. The excellent thing about these locations is that they restock their shelves all the time. That means that you can frequently check these locations for new product. This applies to chain thrift stores like Goodwill and smaller operations. You can also ask them for calendars of their sales dates and when they restock to give yourself a small advantage.

New items in packaging are excellent for reselling. This is fairly common with CDs and DVDs, but other products are also great. Used items are great when there's profit to be made, but new items come with less headaches concerning quality and the potential for customer returns. The best thing about thrift stores is that sometimes the deals are extremely good, meaning that the profit margin is also highly impressive.

Not only can you find obvious items like media and electronics, but sometimes there will be vintage items that can fetch high dollar but be purchased at very low rates.

Yard Sales

Yard sales offer most of the benefits you find in thrift stores, but sometimes they offer even cheaper and wider assortment of items that you can purchase for resale. As with thrift stores, anything in retail packaging still is probably going to be a smart thing to buy.

The best results from yard sales come from taking the time to plan ahead. Not only should you leave early in the morning to get started, but using what you know about the yard sales currently going on in your city, you can map out those that will most likely offer the best products and visit these first. It may take quite a bit of time out of your weekend to go from yard sale to yard sale, but one or two great items can easily make it worth the investment. Just keep in mind that you have competition. There are other people using the same methods to find things to flip, so the quicker you are to get started and find the great items you want to sell, the better your chances. Likewise, going on the first day of the yard sale is ideal. Otherwise, the items will already be picked through.

Yard sales are usually only one or two days, so while they may net better results than thrift stores, they take more time to plan for and may be a bit more hit or miss. These are not repeat opportunities. If you have an idea of items that sell well, you can even ask folks at yard sales if they have anything else they may be willing to let go of at the moment.

Flea Markets

Flea markets typically have a larger amount of products to choose from, and that means a lot of opportunities. There are typically two types of seller at flea markets: those with established booths and moderate prices, and then those that are only there periodically and offer items at more of a yard-sale type of pricing. Both have the potential for earnings, but these temporary sellers are usually going to offer better deals since they may be looking to get rid of as much of their stuff as possible. The greatest thing about flea markets is the sheer amount of sellers. Not only is this great for products, but if you take the time to talk with sellers, you may just pick up some tips and make some new friends that can help you out later.

Craigslist and Facebook Buy/Sell/Trade Groups

Craigslist and Facebook Buy/Sell/Trade groups are like online yard sales. While the prices aren't always as good, there are still opportunities to find great deals. The trick is to be a quick responder when new posts come around. This gives you a chance to offer to pay immediately and possibly get a better price for immediately making the deal. Unfortunately, these sales pages aren't ideal for people that live in remote areas.

Auctions

Your success at auctions can depend on a large number of factors. Needless to say, when the results are good, they're very good. Just be mindful that you're not trying to get wrapped up into a bidding war that could ruin your opportunity for profits. If you're unable to stick to your guns, it is wise to avoid this method. However, large storage locker auctions and other types of large lots that are mostly-blind sales offers the opportunity to buy large amounts of potential products for a very reduced rate. There's a bit of treasure hunting and mystery involved, though, so only go down this route once you have enough capital to justify a loss on taking risks. Whatever you can't sell on eBay can be donated to a thrift store for a tax write-off.

Create Your Own Products

If you are some sort of craftsman, then selling your own products on eBay is a viable option to increase sales. While this sort of thing may not be as easy as finding commonly sold products, smart marketing and working through other sales outlets as well can make for extra profit on something you're already passionate about. This can be anything from woodworking projects, homemade instruments, custom pillows, and pretty much any type of service or product you can think to offer. This may never become your entire business on eBay, but it's an easy way to add extra items for sale.

Wholesale

At some point, if you plan to scale your eBay business up and really make a serious profit, you may have to move into buying products in bulk from wholesalers and selling them at a markup. Wholesale is the key to the concept of buying something for a low price and selling it much higher. If you're willing to put in the work it takes to sell and fulfil a large amount of product, the rewards will be great enough that leaving your day job is a real possibility.

It takes time to handle research and determine which products are truly worth the investment and can be sold in large amounts. A poor decision in product could lead to a loss and a large amount of products sitting around your home or within a storage unit. Never buy anything in bulk on a whim, as this is the easiest way to make a mistake. You need proof that an item will sell well.

The greatest wholesale opportunities are not the easiest to walk into, but by making great relationships with suppliers, you will be given the chance to get great deals on excellent products. A new seller needs to put in some leg work, but it is possible. Most wholesalers are not the manufacturer of the products. Typically, products are manufactured, and the manufacturer sells them in bulk to wholesalers, who then sell in smaller lots to sellers like you.

Not having relationships established with wholesalers doesn't mean you can't find any products in bulk at good prices or begin these relationships. There are wholesalers that are more open to selling smaller amounts.

To find wholesalers, you can:

- **Ask.** It sounds too simple to be true, but the best thing to do is start asking around. Finding a decent wholesaler can be done by contacting manufacturers that make the type of products you want to purchase. By sending them an email and asking them about their wholesalers, they may be willing to provide you with a list of their wholesalers. As you continue this process with other manufacturers, you will begin to notice that some of the same wholesalers appear on many lists. This is a good indication that these wholesalers are worth your time.

- **Online directories** are also available. There are literally hundreds of wholesalers with online websites that allow you to get in contact with them, and directories make it a lot easier to find the ones that might sell the types of products you're interested in buying in bulk. Working directly with wholesalers may be the better method, but this method is open to practically all sellers. Take a look at the following top picks:
  - https://www.doba.com/
  - http://www.wholesalecentral.com/
  - http://alibaba.com
  - http://salehoo.com

- **Trade shows** are an excellent opportunity to network with like-minded individuals and potentially begin a working relationship with wholesalers. If you find a wholesaler's representative, you should be able to get a foot in the door to at least understand what their criteria is for working with small businesses. The more of a people-person you are and the more you can prove your worth to them at the beginning, the easier this becomes. As your reputation improves, so will you chances of meeting people face-to-face at industry events like these trade shows.

Keep in mind that you need to take the time to research a company or directory before you start to work with them or through their platform. Not all of them are 100% legitimate, but that's why we offered you those four directories. They take the time to verify the legitimacy of the companies listing products through their platform, and as a result, it brings a lot more safety on your end.

Small Lots

While we've been discussing large wholesale operations, the truth is that there are some opportunities that may arise where you can purchase a small lot of an item and turn it into profit. In fact, eBay is a great resource for these sorts of lots. By buying in multiples, you receive discounts that are good enough to allow for resell when you sell the item one at a time. It's not as scalable, but it's worth looking into if your capital is still not built up enough to justify larger purchases.

Too Much Work?

With the drive to sell large amounts of product to turn even larger profits comes a few problematic considerations. For one, where exactly are you going to store all of these products? If you live in a large city, there's a good chance that your apartment isn't very spacious. Likewise, if you have a family home but also have children, you may see yourself without a ton of options for large amounts of safe storage. While getting a storage unit is an option, it adds cost to your operations and means you have to frequently travel to the unit before shipping your products.

Perhaps more frustrating is trying to keep up with a large volume of packaging and shipping items. How do you continue to scale if you cannot physically handle all of the work in a day? You could hire employees or put your kids to work, but there are other solutions if you'd rather play a more primary role in your business than "shipper."

Both of these concerns can be solved through dropshipping. Dropshipping is the process of listing products before they're sold and then having the manufacturer or supplier ship them to the customer on your behalf. While you could technically achieve this by listing products and simply having a somewhere to place orders for them, the truth of the matter is that it's much easier if the wholesaler or supplier is willing to help facilitate this process. By allow you to list their products and only selling them to you when you have an order, you eliminate a lot of overhead cost, storage concerns, and the work involved in packaging and shipping orders. We'll discuss this at greater length much later in the book in Chapter 8. I strongly suggest this method if you intend to scale to huge proportions but don't want to open a warehouse.

Keep Looking

The key to product sourcing is to always be on the lookout. If you're spending large amounts of time finding that next product that's going to be a viable seller, this will ensure that your business continues to grow. Now that you've sourced products, what is the next step?

Chapter 5: Listing Your Products

Now that we have setup our eBay account and have our products to sell, it is time to start listing products. This is the step that can make or break your business. Being unprofessional in your listing practices can send a bad message to potential customers. On the other hand, being extremely considerate of the user experience can increase sales dramatically and even allow you to sell items for a bit more than cheaper listings that don't provide as much information.

How to List a Product

Listing a product is a relatively simple process. Let's walk through the product listing process step-by-step to make sure it's easy for you once you're ready to begin listing your products.

Step 1. Check Your Prices

Before listing anything, make sure to take the time to review the prices that your item sells for on eBay. The easiest way to do this is to run a search for the product. Take a look first at what is already listed, especially Buy It

Now listings, as this will give you an idea of your immediate competition's prices. After you write down the lowest price that relates to your item, change your search settings to only display "Sold Items." Taking these sales into account and the values, you'll have a good idea of what you can price your item for and expect to receive. Keep in mind that you will be paying fees on these things.

Step 2. Start Listing

To start a new listing, navigate to eBay.com and in the top-right is a link that reads, "Sell." Click on this link to begin.

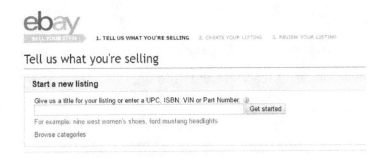

This page will ask you to begin by either writing a title, entering a barcode, ISBN (for books), or other type of identifying number. If you have the barcode or similar information, this can help you automate the process slightly. We'll be using Donkey Kong Country Returns for the Nintendo 3DS as our example. I'm only going to type in "Donkey Kong Country Returns."

This phrase pulls up options for several categories. For items that may fall into many categories, this list can be much longer. Once you select the appropriate category, you can continue.

Because eBay has this item in its database, I can click the "Sell yours" button under the product description. If the item you're selling isn't on the list, you can choose "Continue with your listing" to create the listing instead.

Step 3. Fill in the Condition

Product details

- Game Name: Donkey KONG Country Returns 3D
- Genre: Action/Adventure
- Platform: Nintendo 3DS
- Release Year: 2013
- Rating: E-Everyone

See details | ☑ Include the product information in your listing | Look for a different product in the catalog

Describe your item   Add or remove options | Get help

* Title
Donkey Kong Country Returns 3D (Nintendo 3DS, 2013)

* Condition
-   ▼

* Add photos
Upload up to 12 photos that show your item in multiple views (such as front, back, side, and close-up). You are required to have a minimum of 1 photo in your list
Try our new enhanced photo uploader Add/edit photos | Classic uploader   Remove all photos

Stock Photo 1

Because eBay already has some information on this product, it will load some of the details on my behalf, but there are still a lot of things we can change.

First, we may want to use a different title. We'll discuss this and writing the description separately in a few pages.

For now, let's focus on "Condition." When choosing condition, consider the following choices:

- **Brand New.** This must be a brand new item with no damage. That means if the item comes in shrink wrap, the shrink wrap is still on it. Do NOT list anything as Brand New if this doesn't apply.

- **Like New.** If it's basically brand new but not in original packaging or shrink wrap, then it can be listed as "Like New." It needs to be MINT condition.

- **Very Good.** Used items that are still very much intact and functional may be listed as "Very Good" condition. For movies, music, or video games, this means the original case is still included. The case must be in excellent condition, not just the media. This is for items with very minor wear but otherwise complete.

- **Good.** These items are clearly in used condition but they are still functional. If there is minor damage or scuffs, that is okay as long as everything works and is complete.

- **Acceptable.** Works well but may be missing some parts, such as liner notes for records or CDs, cases for video games, etc.

In some categories, the only options for condition are "New" and "Used." This should go without saying, but "New" items need to fit the "Brand New" condition described above. Used items are everything else.

Step 4. Add Photos

You must include at least one image. In our example, it automatically adds the stock photograph, but it is not advised to use stock photographs unless it cannot be helped. Take the time to take clear pictures that paint a reliable picture of what the buyer will receive should they win your auction or purchase your listing. You can upload pictures from your computer's hard drive or through your phone if you're setting up listings on a mobile device. You may have a maximum of 12 pictures total, so take advantage of these and try to offer 12 images when it's practical. Pictures are a huge part of selling well, so skimping on this is not advised.

Step 5. Add Specifics

In some categories, you may be asked to provide specific details. These specifics are optional, but if you know the information or believe it will add to the listing, then take the time to fill in these additional pieces of data. For our example, it asks for things like "subgenre," publisher, compatible features, etc. I would doubt that this would help me sell the product, so I'll skip it. However, your product may benefit from more information. You can also add in your own item specifics if you want, but this is only advised for items that you'll be selling for a high price or in bulk.

Step 6. Add Description

Next, you'll add in the description. We'll discuss this in more detail soon, but for now, just consider that it's better to keep it simple than try to overuse the many features for design that are available. This is a critical part of selling, so do not skip out on writing a full description. A one-sentence description that says, "works well, best game ever," is not sufficient.

Step 7. Add Price

Next, we'll add in our price and determine the listing style. You can choose between an "Auction" or a "Fixed Price" listing. With an auction, you can also offer a fixed price for people to purchase the item without going through the auction trouble, and this Buy It Now price lasts as long as the bid is less than 50% of the fixed price you've set.

In this section, you also decide on the duration of your listing. For most auctions, 7 days is a smart amount of time. For fixed priced listings, 30 days is the standard, and there's the option to automatically relist items until they sell. Note that relisting an item takes one of your free listing credits. I suggest using these two figures because they are typically going to be free and not incur additional listing fees.

You can also take this opportunity to make this a charity auction.

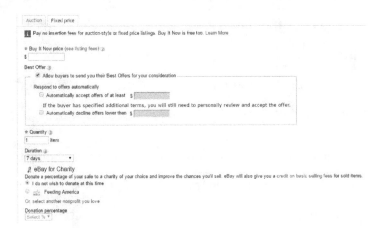

If you want to post a fixed price listing, you will see a slightly different setup. There is also the option in the fixed price listing style to have the "Best Offer" feature activated. With this feature, potential customers are able to offer you a price for your item, and you'll be given the chance to counteroffer. You can setup eBay to automatically reject an offer that's too low or automatically accept an offer that you're willing to take, or you can manually respond to these requests.

Additionally with the fixed price listings, you are able to list more than one of a product. So if you have 10 to sell, you can easily change the quantity. I'd typically change the duration to 30 days at least, but it's up to you how long you want a listing to remain active. You can always reactive ones that finish if you want, but it's ideal to keep it live as long as possible if you want there to be notices on eBay that let potential customers know that hundreds of the item have been sold to happy customers!

For many of us, fixed price Buy It Now listings are going to work better for our business. Auctions are best reserved for lots with multiple items, rare or antique items, and similarly unusual situations. Auctions offer the opportunity for either losses or exceeding the amount you'd normally sell a product at. There's a risk involved.

Step 8. Setup Shipping

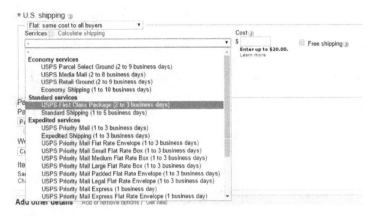

Next, we'll setup our shipping costs and methods. In my account, I have it setup to default to USPS, but you can change this with the "Add or remove options" link.

I always offer Free Shipping, especially on items that ship relatively cheap to begin with. Honestly, the only time you shouldn't use free shipping option is if the item is extremely heavy, and even then, it's often better to just work the shipping cost into your initial price. When choosing free shipping, you can skip inputting all of these additional details. If you insist on ignoring my advice and want to input calculated shipping, our example of a video game would ship First-Class, and it would weigh about 12 ounces with a package size of 6" x 9" x 2".

Under the "handling time" drop box, we really want to choose "1 business day" if it is at all possible for us to ship every business day. (This is required for Power Seller Status, which we'll discussed in Chapter 3.) If it isn't possible to ship this often, then make sure to choose the appropriate amount of time between purchase and shipping for your business needs. Quicker times help improve your visibility on eBay.

Step 9. Add Additional Details

Finally, we'll add the last details to your listing. There are a few items in this section, so let's cover them one by one.

With sales tax, you really only need to charge this if your state requires it. Check your local laws and ask your legal representative about this before deciding. For most of us, we can get away without charging sales tax.

Returns should be accepted. If you have any goal of becoming a full-fledged eBay-based business, you really need to offer returns. The truth of the matter is that eBay makes it easy for customers to force you to accept returns anyway, so offering them ahead of time saves you the hassle. It is my advice to accept returns for 30 days. This sends a positive message that you're easy to work with, and it also helps you gain Power Seller status on eBay, which will add a few tools/benefits to your repertoire as a seller.

It is up to you whether you charge restocking fees for buyers that decide to return items for reasons other than damage or unexpected issues. This helps reduce loss of time and capital involved in selling an item, but it can also deter some buyers.

Step 10. Click "Submit Listing"

And that's all there is to it! Your listing is now live, and within an hour or less people will be able to see your item when they run searches on eBay or browse by category. Next, we'll back track a little bit and discuss titles and descriptions in a little more depth.

How to Write Your Product Description

Writing your product description is probably the most important part of running a successful eBay business. The listing should explain thoroughly what the customer will receive in exchange for their money. It should include all the relevant details possible to express, and it should be well-written. If you struggle with grammar, it is advised to find a proofreader to help you out, especially if you're going to be selling hundreds of the same item and have a listing that lasts months on end for this reason.

Titles

Use keywords that best describe your listing. Consider how people are going to be searching for your item, and potentially even take the time to run a search for the same item yourself to see what keywords they are using within their titles. The title should first and foremost explain what the item is, but past that, it can include additional words to help. Things to include might be:

- Brand and model name – be specific
- Size and color, when applicable
- Category your item is in (if not obvious from brand/model name)

Things to avoid include:

- Don't use words like "LOOK!" or "WOW!"
- Avoid the use of all caps.
- Synonyms aren't going to help you sell items that well, so avoid them.
- Punctuation is unneeded.
- Any false information. If the item is broken, it should be advertised as broken.
- Avoid phone numbers, email addresses, or website addresses – the only exception here is when you are selling domain names, but that's not something we'll discuss.

- Avoid words like "banned" or "prohibited." If an item truly is banned or prohibited, you wouldn't be able to sell it on eBay. This is a false marketing technique.

- Don't use brand names or artist names that aren't part of the listing.

Take the time to review the titles of other seller's items with the same products for sale. This will give you a good idea of what is working and what isn't going to work for you. Do not copy their verbatim, as this doesn't help you stand out at all.

Description

Writing the description may be one of the toughest part of listing items for sale on eBay. Not only does it need to be presented well with relatively good grammar, but it needs to include all the pertinent information about your product in a way that helps it stand out amongst all the other options.

When writing, make sure to segment information into separate paragraphs, possible under headings, that way the information is easy to digest. One long paragraph for a listing is difficult to read and may actually push buyers away from your products.

Focus on the most important information first. This means the item details, color, the condition, etc.

Be very specific. You need to let customers know about sizes, colors, when a product was made, who made it, and any other features that are really pivotal to your product.

Make sure that the reader understands exactly what is included when they purchase the item. This should also be reflected in the photos, so when you're taking pictures, make sure to only picture what is included and make sure all items included are in images.

The easier and more useful this description, the better you are setup to make the sale. Be sure to mention your returns and shipping policies as well, but place this at the very end to avoid clogging up information about the product.

Adding some creative flair to your description is a great idea. Being creative or funny, telling a story about the item, is going to help encourage people to make the purchase. Trying to make some small connection to the potential customer goes a long way.

Always be sure to avoid the following things in your descriptions:

- Any information that simply isn't true. The better you can describe the item, the easier it is to avoid buyer's remorse, returns, and refund requests that can hurt your overall business and lead to bad feedback if not mitigated well. If an item is refurbished, do not try to call it "New."

- Don't embed images too often. You can upload images to the listing itself, so use that method to show the potential customer your product.

- Avoid adding a lot of information that isn't relevant to the item for sale. While a quick note about having other similar items may be wise, spending half your description on these things is not going to have a great impact. Plus, you'll be wasting your own time.

- Avoid heavy use of formatting, font choices, and colors. Simple is better! Not only does it allow for easier access on mobile devices, such as smart phones and tablets, but it also ensures that nothing is distracting to the reading experience.

- Don't use any copy/pasted materials. This is not wise. Not only does it hurt your visibility on search engines, but it usually won't sound organic with your other material.

- Don't be negative. While there are frustrations involved in being an ecommerce entrepreneur, this isn't your place to voice them. Do not complain about other buyers, and do not give a list of demands required to be a buyer. This will scare people off. If you're difficult to buy from, then it goes to reason you'll be difficult to work with should something with my order go wrong.

- Don't use copyrighted or trademarked materials. That's illegal. There are other things prohibited by eBay as well, which you can learn about here: http://pages.ebay.com/help/policies/items-ov.html

Example Listing

Below is an example of a high-quality listing written for a video game being sold. It contains personality and practicality.

Title: Donkey Kong Country Returns – Nintendo 3DS – Mint Condition

Description:

This side-scrolling adventure game was developed as a reimagined experience of fans of the original Donkey Kong Country series, making it perfect for new and old players alike. With new enemies, levels, and power-ups, it's sure to please everyone.

You are bidding on a like-new, opened game that comes with the original case, instructions, and game disc. Playable on Nintendo 3DS and New 3DS. The condition is truly mint. Other than testing it to ensure it played as expected... and maybe because it's just too fun not to try out... I'm unsure if anyone has ever actually played this copy. I'd keep it if I didn't already have a copy!

I accept returns for any reason up to 30 days, and I'm eager to help you should there be any problems with your order. Contact me with any questions or concerns.

Find more video games by checking out my other listings. I have listed hundreds of games, movies, records, and books! Fast and free shipping is my way of saying thank you for your business!

That's a nice, simple listing with a little bit of information, a little bit of personality, and clear explanation of what the buyer receives, how returns are accepted, and how shipping is handled.

Proofread

Once you've written out your description, it is ideal to take the time to re-read it once or twice and tighten up the language, remove unwanted errors, and possibly add some detail that slipped by you the first go around. While you want to make this process quick, taking the time to check your work shows an attention to detail that isn't lost on customers.

Update Your Listings

Lastly, once and awhile, it may be wise to take some time to review listings that have been active for a long period of time and simply update the language, add new details, etc. Taking the time to improve your work overtime will help ensure you're providing the best possible experience for potential customers.

Chapter 6: Shipping Sold Products

Putting in the effort to plan a system of managing your inventory and shipping your products ahead of time will help avoid the pitfalls of a disorganized business, selling products you no longer have to sell, and the bad feedback that results, all things that can cripple your business. In terms of shipping, the best method is to be over-prepared.

Postage Scale

The first thing you want to do is purchase a postage scale that can weigh packages up to 50 pounds or more. Having a reliable postage scale makes it possible to weigh all of your packages and pay exact shipping costs only. It also helps avoid incorrect postage issues that can delay packages.

If you plan to charge exact shipping costs, you can weigh your item before packaging and shipping them. Because boxes and packing material will add to the weight a little bit, you may want to either package the item prior to weighing or simply add a bit of extra weight on eBay to help cover this additional cost.

If you are going to offer free shipping on your items, you can simply wait to weigh your packages until after they are sold. Just keep in mind that you will want to price the item high enough to cover the cost of shipping and help you make a profit.

Postage Supplies

You will need postage supplies. It is often wise to have some on hand. Not only are these things cheaper to buy in bulk, but it also saves you a lot of time, especially if you use package pickup with USPS. You will need several things, including:

- Bubble mailers in multiple sizes. These are perfect for smaller items that don't require the sturdy protection of a cardboard box. The reduced weight helps keep down the cost of shipping and sometimes allow for items to placed in a mailbox rather than on a porch or other accessible area.

- Cardboard boxes, in multiple sizes. Cardboard boxes are ideal for fragile materials and larger items. Cardboard boxes come in practically any sizes, and with a little bit of work and a box cutter, most of them can be cut down to fix your item better and reduce the weight and therefore the cost is reduced. In some cases for extra fragile items, it is wise to double box them and take the hit on shipping cost. The only thing worse than overpaying for shipping is an item being broken while traveling in the post. Even if it's not really your fault, you are responsible for damaged goods. Even if you have a no-returns policy, which you should never have, eBay may force you to accept a return or offer a refund for items that don't arrive as expected.

- Bubble wrap. Bubble wrap is a must for fragile items, and it is my advice to always use bubble wrap even on less fragile items. You can save bubble wrap from packages you receive to help cut down costs a bit, but buying in bulk is the best way to get bang for your buck.

- Newspaper can be used for padding, but it is important to consider that it doesn't really protect anything from getting broken, it just stops it from moving around as much in the box.

- Printer paper or adhesive shipping labels for printing your labels off of eBay.

- Tape. Pretty much any shipping tape works, but larger orders are going to be cheaper. You are going to need a lot of tape, so it doesn't serve you well to buy it at the corner store every other day.

Shipping Methods

EBay will walk you through the shipping process for using their labels. It is advised to take advantage of their shipping tools because it comes with a discounted rate you won't receive at the post office. There are several shipping methods, and here are the ones you'll most likely be using:

- First class. First class mail applies to anything at 16 ounces or less. It doesn't matter if it's a box or envelope, as long as it weighs in under 16 ounces after it is packaged and has a label on it, it can be sent first class. First class mail usually ships within a few days, and it always costs less than $4 to ship a first-class package.

- Media mail. Media mail is only to be used for educational and media items like books, records, CDs, and DVDs. A stack of unburned CD-Rs does not count as media mail, and any type of media with heavy use of advertisements is also not allowed. Media mail allows for a very cheap price even on heavy items, but the shipping time is generally much slower. If you are caught trying to ship items media mail that do not qualify, you may be charged extra. One downside to media mail is that mail forwarding isn't included, meaning if someone changes addresses before they receive the item you ship, they'll be forced to pay postage.

- Parcel mail. Parcel mail is for heavier items and larger packages. The costs vary depending on location, but the speed is generally slow. Parcel mail is rarely going to be the best method of shipping for an eBay seller, so only use it if the cost is significantly less than priority mail.

- Priority. Priority mail typically ships in 2-3 days, and the price is generally going to be close to parcel mail, though it can vary based on location if you're not using a priority mail box. Priority boxes come in a number of sizes, from small, medium, large, and several envelop sizes. These boxes are free from the USPS; you can even go to their website and have some delivered to your home. When shipping a flat-rate box, the price is the same no matter where it's going in the United States. When shipping a non-priority box, local shipping will be relatively inexpensive, but shipping across the country becomes pricey very quickly.

While you can also ship with UPS or FedEx or other carriers, working through the USPS is generally the best method unless an item requires freight. I do not recommend working with items so large that they must be shipped via freight delivery. This is more headache than it's worth, and most buyers will have an issue with the high costs involved in just shipping an item.

Shipping Tips

1. Include a thank you note. A small thank you note is a smart way to encourage customers to leave you positive feedback or reach out to you with any issues prior to leaving negative feedback. This can also encourage buyers to visit your website if you have one.

2. Ship quickly. Shipping as soon as possible is an ideal way to get the best possible customer feedback. Additionally, those that process shipments within one day will be able to reach "Top Rated Seller" status much easier.

3. Offer free shipping and build the cost into your prices. Because one of the way people can search is to only look at free shipping options, this small tip will help you dramatically increase the views on your listings, and it can quite likely be the difference in making a sale and not making a sale.

4. Package everything well. Do not skimp on bubble wrap and padding for your packages. A poorly packaged item shows a lack of care, and that will not be lost on a buyer, especially if the product comes broken. There are buyers that are particular about how they receive their items, so be on top of your game.

5. When possible, ship items together. If one person buys more than one item, then it makes sense to ship them together to save on the costs. If this isn't possible (very fragile item with another heavy item), then make sure to let your buyer know ahead of time that they will receive two separate packages to ensure the best possible experience and no confusion.

6. Include a packing slip, especially with higher priced items. This isn't required, but it can be an easy way to show your professionalism to buyers. This is especially ideal if you are selling higher priced items. A receipt of the transaction is common in most retail operations, so it shouldn't be overlooked in your operations either.

How to Ship After a Sale

Once an item has sold, you should receive an item notifying you. Following the link to ship on this page will take you to the form required, but if for some reason the payment hasn't come through after the sale or you lose the email, we'll discuss how to manually go into eBay and find everything you need to print your labels.

Step 1. Log in.

Log in at eBay.com. Once logged in, there should be a "My eBay" link in the top right-hand corner. Hovering you mouse over this, you'll be given a menu. From this menu, select "Selling."

Step 2. Go to Sold items.

On the next page, you'll see a long navigation menu on the left-hand side of the page. Scroll down until you see, "Sold" and select this.

Step 3. Start the Process of Print Shipping Label

On this new page, you can choose the item you have sold and want to print a label for. On the right-hand side will be a "More Actions" link, and when you click this, a menu pops up that includes "Print Shipping Label." Click this option.

Step 4. Select a Carrier

Next, you can select a carrier. For most of us, this is likely to be USPS. You will be redirected to the form required to create the shipping label.

Step 5. Input Details

On this form, you'll input all the details about weight and type of shipping being used. Make sure to know the approximate length, width, and height of any boxes, and have the weight ready. You will have the chance to add additional services like insurance, delivery confirmation, signature requirements, etc.

Step 6. Print the Label

Check that all of your information is correct, and if it is, click "Print Shipping Label." It will bring up your printer's dialog box. Make sure you select the correct printer and have paper or adhesive labels already loaded into the printer. Once the label is printed, all you have to do is attach it to the box and ship it. If you're using plain paper, try not to cover up the barcode with tape, as this can sometimes make it difficult to scan for postal carriers.

The tracking number generated is automatically passed on to your buyer if you purchase postage through eBay/PayPal, so there's no need to type this in. If you ship manually instead of using eBay labels, be sure to keep the tracking number and input this into eBay later.

That's All Folks!

That's really all there is to it. After you tape the label on your box, you an setup a USPS pickup from USPS.com, or you can take them to the post office yourself that same day or the day after. It is advised to start using package pickups because you'll want to ship everything the next day. It is my advice to take care of your mailman! This means leaving gifts for holidays, offering them waters if you're home while they're working in hot weather, etc. This may not truly impact your business, but you're going to be adding a lot of work to their day, so it's the least you can do. And it never hurts to have a good relationship with the person handling your packages!

Chapter 7: Opening an eBay Store

EBay stores are ideal when you wish to target a specific niche. While eBay stores may not be the absolute best solution for an ecommerce standalone store, it does offer the safety and promotion that makes eBay such an excellent place to sell your products. (It also expands the amount of listings you can have without paying an insertion fee.) For those that have a niche that they're passionate about or have found a type of product that regularly sells well, then an eBay store can be setup to help reduce some of the fees and costs associated with listings and final value costs.

What Type of Store?

There are three levels of eBay stores:

- **Basic eBay Store**
  $25/month or $20/month with a full year subscription
  0.20 cent fixed price insertion fees, 0.25 cent auction insertion fees
  Final value fees between 3.5%-9.15%

250 free fixed price listings per month

250 free auction listings per month

$25 quarterly eBay-branded shipping supplies coupon

$30 quarterly additional promoted listing credits

5,000 monthly marketing and promotion emails

Requirements:

Have an eBay account with a verified PayPal account

Ideal for those that list roughly 250 listings per month or often list high dollar items and want the discounted fees to help them make the most of their sales.

- **Premium eBay Store**

  $75/month or $60/month with a full year subscription

  0.10 cent fixed price insertion fees, 0.15 cent auction insertion fees

  Final value fees between 3.5%-9.15%

  1000 free fixed price listings per month

500 free auction listings per month

$50 quarterly eBay-branded shipping supplies coupon

$30 quarterly additional promoted listing credits

7,500 monthly marketing and promotion emails

Selling Manager Pro subscription at no extra cost

Requirements:

EBay account with verified PayPal account, and it must not have a below standard performance rating. Learn about seller standards at http://pages.ebay.com/help/policies/seller-non-performance.html.

Ideal for those that list more than 1,000 items per month.

- **Anchor eBay Store**

  $350/month or $300/month with a full year subscription

  0.05 cent fixed price insertion fees, 0.10 cent auction insertion fees

Final value fees between 3.5%-9.15%

10,000 free fixed price listings per month

1,000 free auction listings per month

$150 quarterly eBay-branded shipping supplies coupon

$25 quarterly promotional listing credits

$30 quarterly additional promoted listing credits

10,000 monthly marketing and promotion emails

Dedicated customer support

Requirements:

EBay account with verified PayPal account, and it must not have a below standard performance rating. Learn about seller standards at http://pages.ebay.com/help/policies/seller-non-performance.html.

Ideal for those that list 10,000 items per month and want the best possible savings and customer service available for eBay sellers.

Find Your Niche

Again, the trick with eBay stores is that they work best for focused types of products. While you could sell multiple categories, creating a store that is targeted at a specific demographic, hobby, or section of a market allows for the best possible results from marketing opportunities. Becoming a reputable source for a single niche allows for growth that selling just any items that come up doesn't.

You can start with a single type of product and expand into items that fit similar interests and uses. For example, if you sell comic books, you could expand to video games and other related collectibles. Otherwise, you're running something that feels a lot like a yard sale, which defeats the purpose of opening a standalone store in the first place.

After you've been selling on eBay for a while, you may have an idea of the type of products that you are good at selling, sourcing, and feel passionate about. This makes for easy niche selection. But if you're completely unsure which niche to approach, it may be time to do some research.

Write down 10 categories (with plenty of products) that you are passionate about. For example, if you're interested in building models, then the "hobby" niche might be for you. From here, you can research the niches further through Google. See who the competitors are, learn some of the best-selling items, and learn if there seems to be a large following that is interested in these niches. Choosing becomes easier when there appears to be a market for these things.

If you're unsure if your niche has any selling power, consider some of the products you'd like to sell and do some research on them through eBay. The ideal situation is that you will be able to see that these items sell even outside of eBay stores. While a store may allow you to sell a few items that are less commonly sold, since someone browsing it is likely interested in the entire niche, having items that can sell consistently are the key to being successful on platforms like eBay.

While there are many other ways to help choose a niche, the best approach is always something you love. If you love it, it will be much easier to generate buzz and great content to go along with your product listings.

Customize Your Store

One of the great things about opening an eBay store is the ability to design the store and allow it to operate as a standalone from all the hubbub of auctions and fixed price listings (even though it will technically just be a bunch of fixed priced listings). After you've paid for a package, you'll be given the ability to design a storefront.

The design that goes into your store should match your niche as well as possible. While a simple design may fit almost any niche, taking the time for small improvements will go a long way. When naming your store and writing content, take into consideration the use of keywords that will help search engines find your store and make them visible to people searching for similar products and information online. While it may be tempting to use a name that sounds unique, the truth is that something as simple as, "Best Value Comic Books, Magic the Gathering, and More" tends to rank better than "Bob's Comics."

Incorporate your niche into your logo design to help keep people interested. The more involved you are within the niche (i.e. not just a seller, but an actual fan), the better results you should expect from people that may come across your store. This is one of the reasons finding a niche you are actually passionate about can help you be successful on eBay.

List Items Professionally

We spoke earlier about how to list items and how important things like images, well-written descriptions, and informative titles can be. This becomes even more true with eBay stores, especially if you decide to list some items that may not be quick sellers. The better your content, the easier it is for people to find your products and the easier it is for them to commit to buying from you.

Always be honest and upfront in your listings. Trying to hide defects is pointless and can only hurt your reputation on eBay, or at the very least cause several costly refunds or replacements. When starting an eBay Store, the importance of high-quality output becomes even more serious for your success.

Promoting Your Store

One of the things that an eBay store affords is a better opportunity to promote your business. With single listings, it can be difficult to promote yourself. Where would you send people? To single auctions or fixed item listings? To your "See Seller's Other Items" page? That would look awfully unflattering for your business. Having a store allows you to point people to a dedicated storefront that appears professional, organizes your listings, and lays out the policies that you operate with.

Email lists are a great way to promote your store. Customers that have bought from you and like the type of items you post may be willing to sign up for an email list. As we mention when describing the different store options, eBay integrates off-site email marketing into these programs. Take advantage of them.

Social media is a great way to begin connecting with people that share your interest (or the interests of your niche). Finding likeminded people is not only great for business, but if you are truly passionate about the subject matter, then it will also be personally rewarding and easy to connect with your personal customers.

If you run a website or a blog, then this is another obvious place to tell others about your store. You can expand this by giving insight into how you choose which products are best, doing reviews, and making the blog a general resource that people find great value in. These things can directly translate into sales for your business.

We'll discuss more promotional ideas in Chapter 10, and most of them apply to your eBay Store.

Subscribing to eBay Stores

To subscribe to one of these packages, just log into your eBay account and navigate to http://pages.ebay.com/seller-center/stores/subscriptions.html

From here, eBay will walk you through the process. Just keep in mind that you need to retain great seller ratings to maintain a store. This is not for someone just testing eBay out, and it should be a step up after you've started to find yourself sticking to a niche.

Chapter 8: Dropshipping Method

During the section on how to source products, we mentioned the option of using a dropshipping method to expand your business. We held off on explaining this too much because it deserves a lot of consideration. Additionally, I believe it helpful for first-time entrepreneurs to learn their business inside-out, and that can only be done by at least getting their toes wet in handling every aspect on their own, especially something as time-consuming as shipping when you're a successful one-man operation or small team.

Once you find a method of sourcing products that provides consistent results, moving to dropshipping should be a fairly simple process. By now you're comfortable working with suppliers, and you've also nailed how to determine if an opportunity is worth the time and effort. But if you aim to remain a small operation and continue scaling large scale, then going the route of dropshipping is what will eliminate a huge amount of your workload.

Dropshipping is a fairly simple concept. Rather than purchasing products in bulk from a supplier, you work with the wholesaler or manufacturer to have them shop items only after you've sold them. The process goes like this:

1. You list a product that your suppliers sell on eBay.
2. Someone buys that product.
3. You place an order for the product and have it shipped directly to the buyer.
4. Your supplier ships this item for you.
5. You are responsible for any customer service or issues that arise.

This helps keep down your overhead costs since you won't actually have any stock, and it allows you to scale your business to sell thousands and thousands of items if you want. It is large volumes that accounts for high earnings, as the cost per product is higher than traditional wholesaling methods. However, you're also not paying for shipping materials, you aren't spending time packaging items, and you aren't spending time shipping items. All this freed up time allows you to focus on sourcing new dropshipped products, writing great descriptions, and improving your business in other ways. The key is great product selection and finding good suppliers to work with. This is singlehanded the best method to scale into a very large business without creating a large body of employees.

Of course, not everything about dropshipping is great. As mentioned, you are still the contact point with customer service issues. If something arrives broken, or defective, or it's not even the right item to begin with, then you have to serve a middleman between the buyer and the supplier. This is one of the reasons having decent suppliers is helpful. For this reason, when it's possible, it's smart to buy at least one or two of every item and take the time to make sure it's quality lives up to the glowing description you're about to write for it. Selling something just because it's cheap can end up landing you some bad feedback.

Being able to keep tabs on the stock available for any given product also becomes tenfold more difficult, as you can only take the suppliers word for it, and if you're selling thousands of items it difficult to spend your time check on the inventory amount of each item. Once again, you'll have to play the customer service expert and explain that an order has to be canceled because *you* are out of stock. Again, it's your fault, not the suppliers.

Part of the difficulty of staying organized is that you will likely be working with several suppliers. Not only does this make it difficult to understand inventory issues before they're issues, but it also means that should a customer order two items that come from different suppliers, then they'll receive those items separately. The standard is usually to ship items together if you can.

These things don't mean that dropshipping is a waste of time. On the contrary, the sheer scalability of the model means that someone who is great at customer service and sourcing products will be able to grow exponentially compared to trying to handle these other tasks on their own.

The important thing to remember is that you can't sell horrible items and you can't work with irresponsible suppliers that don't ship packages with proper protections in place. That's why it's suggested to always order one or two of a product before even listing it.

Suppliers that Offer Dropshipping

Many companies offer or claim to offer dropshipping services. The first thing to note is that there are several dropshipping scams. There are two really obvious signs that this opportunity might be worth skipping:

- Monthly fees are uncommon with legitimate suppliers. They should be making money on your orders, not on monthly fees.
- They sell products to anybody. Chances are that they're offer these for the same prices and you'll basically be ordering from a "dropshipping" service that's actually just a retail operation.

Additionally, even legitimate suppliers that may offer dropshipping for their customers will have an initial minimum order of $500. The best piece of advice here is to either buy $500 worth of product that you can sell and ship on your own, or offer to put down a $500 deposit that they will use as a credit. This should only be done with companies you have reason to trust, but it is a simple way to gain their trust and have them take your business seriously.

When it's possible, working directly with a manufacturer is ideal because they can offer the absolute best rates per product. Wholesalers are more likely to be the suppliers we'll be working with most the time. Initially finding suppliers can be difficult, but there are several methods you can utilize:

- **Google searches** are an obvious place to start. However, wholesalers are notorious for having websites with awful designs. This is NOT a sign that they are illegitimate businesses or untrustworthy. Likewise, they don't utilize very good search engine optimization techniques a lot of times, so it may be third or fourth pages of results with some legitimate wholesalers still showing up.

- **Trade shows and similar events.** Sometimes, you can simply attend the types of events that fit the products and stuff you are interested in selling. Doing this, you can make connections with several people, hopefully someone that will help you by letting you know their supplier or if they are a supplier, will want to work with you. Networking in general is wise in business, even online eBay businesses.

- **Check out your competition.** If you find a seller that has the type of products you like to list on eBay, you can order from them in hopes that their supplier's address is on the package and not theirs. Likewise, you can ask them! They may not tell you, but it can't hurt.

- **Ask manufacturer.** Only a small number of manufacturers are willing to take the time to dropship items for small businesses, but many of them will offer you a list of wholesalers they work with. Once you have these lists, you can determine which names come up often. Those are probably the best wholesalers to begin working with.

- **Wholesale directories.** Some wholesale directories will check out their entries, but not all of them are well maintained. As such, be sure to exercise caution. A few safer choices include:
    - http://worldwidebrands.com
    - http://salehoo.com

- http://doba.com
- http://aliexpress.com

Before Making the Call

Before you start ringing up local wholesalers and asking them questions, there are a number of tasks you can complete that will make it easier to get their respect and business. Some wholesalers may actually require these things be true before they even consider working with you. Tasks you may need to complete first:

- **Register your business.** While you could just call yourself a sole proprietor and sell on eBay, if you intend to work some wholesalers, you likely want to register your business. Many will register as an LLC, but you should discuss this with your financial and legal advisers. The thing is that these B2B (business-to-business) companies want to work with legitimate businesses. Investing in a new client is best when there's reason to believe they'll be repeat customers.

- **Be humble.** You are new to this industry, and having a lot of demands is not a good way to network or achieve anything. Build your relationships before asking for huge discounts.

- **Be established.** This may not be required for all wholesalers, but many will treat you much better if you can show them that you're established somehow. For an eBay seller, this may mean you already have thousands of feedback from your own work. If you only go the route of dropshipping, this will mean working with suppliers that may not offer the best prices but are more open to new sellers. If you appear serious, they will take you a lot more serious. So be serious and be established. This is a job, after all.

Choosing Products for Dropshipping

If you've taken the time to build a business outside of dropshipping, then you probably have a good idea of how to choose what new products to sell. If you haven't done this, you have a bit of a learning process to go through in choosing the best products. While you'll likely be selling some cheaper products, the ideal products are going to be over $100 and allow for quite a bit of markup so you can produce a decent profit.

Once you have suppliers that agree to offer dropshipping services to you, the next step is researching their products in more depth. If you can find similar products for sale on eBay, you can determine a reasonable selling price and thus determine if you will make a profit after taking fees and shipping costs into account. The plus side is that you aren't spending money on these products, so even if they don't sell well, it's only time that you've spent, not a lot of overhead on a stockpile of items you are having a hard time selling.

If you have found some products that you have a reason to believe will net you a decent profit, it is now time to put in the effort to write great descriptions and titles.

While some working a dropshipping business will simply copy and paste these descriptions and images from the manufacturer, this is a horrible idea that will hurt your business. Taking the time to write excellent descriptions helps your listings become easier to find on search engines and stand out to readers and potential customers. It is ideal to take images a well, as stock images are obviously stock images, and many customers are going to avoid these type of pictures and products.

We've mentioned it before, but it is truly wise to take the time to order the products that you plan to sell. Not only does this allow you take your own images of the item, but it allows you to make sure the quality is consistent. What I like to do is order at least two of each item, that way I can tell if these two are the same or slightly difference from one another. From there, I test the items to help me find their usefulness and write a great description about the item. Checking items for their quality level ensures that your customers are receiving only products that you would personally be happy to own. While you can skip this step and still make great money and pull products once you have complaints, it is my belief that having only the best products from the start is best for reputation. Once you're done testing items, you can sell them on eBay on your own for a little profit.

Even once you've worked with the same supplier with several products without any issues, I still prefer to do these tests because it helps me write and it allows me to take my own images. Having my own images help me stand out if other people are dropshipping the same product and only using manufacturer images for them. Of course, if test products are consistently low quality from a supplier, it's time to leave that supplier in the dust.

Although there are many hurdles to jump over with dropshipping, the monetary investments are fairly minimal compared to the time investments. So if you make a mistake, it's not a mistake that leads to a huge loss. You just keep trying with new products until you find some that work.

Research Is Key

Once your business grows so large that it is impossible to handle shipping on your own or without a large crew, then going the route of dropshipping is your best way to move forward if you wish to keep your business small but continue your growth. Taking the time to research products, research potential suppliers, and research what products are about to be trending is the leg up you need to make the dropshipping method work best in your favor. The good news is that if your approach is to list large amounts of products, you're sure to see enough success to justify the work. As you work on high numbers, you'll effectively be researching. It's the long way around, but for some just diving in is the best way to learn.

Chapter 9: Tips and Tricks

This chapter is simple a list of tips and tricks to keep in mind while you're working on your eBay business. There are many small details about eBay, some more anecdotal than fact, but there is still some truth to be found in the experiences of others. Based on our knowledge, these following points are important to know when trying to navigate your eBay journey.

Selling Internationally

Selling internationally can be a hassle, but it doesn't have to be. For the simplest method, you can utilize eBay's Global Shipping Program by simply selecting this in your shipping preferences while you're creating a new listing.

The Global Shipping Program works by having you send a package to a USA fulfilment center after an international customer buys it. From there, the fulfilment center handles everything from customs to getting the product to the customer. EBay will automatically add any customs fees and additional shipping to the customer's order, and you'll simply spend the same amount you'd spend on shipping any other item without ever seeing anything about these added costs.

While the Global Shipping Program does have added fees for buyers, most are willing to pay these because many products are difficult to procure overseas through other methods. This simplified method of selling internationally is excellent if you don't want to add a lot of headache but want to be able to offer your products internationally.

How to Avoid Problems with Transactions

One of the biggest keys to being successful on eBay is reducing the amount of issues customers have with your services. There are a few things you can keep in mind to make this possible. These include:

- Accurate listings that don't hide defects and have images that show exactly what the buyer should expect when they receive the product.
- Fair shipping prices and fast shipping, as customers are not happy to pay inflated rates and want their items as soon as possible. Quick

shipping is a huge perk when trying to retain positive feedback.

- Always offer PayPal. Don't even consider listing anything and not accepting PayPal payments. Not only are most eBay users also using PayPal, but even if they aren't, PayPal can process all other types of payments as well, including credit card and debit cards.

- Always provide a tracking number. Not only does this show the item is actually being shipped, but if it should get lost in the post, it makes it much easier to track down and remedy the situation later.

- Never ship before a payment posts. This should go without saying, but some fraudulent buyers on eBay try to buy items, never pay, and receive them before closing down their accounts and disappearing forever.

What Happens When Someone Doesn't Pay?

In the event that someone doesn't pay in a few days following an auction or fixed price listing, there are a few things to keep an eye out for. This includes:

- Is the eBay account still active? If it isn't, you should file a case immediately with eBay.

- If they are still active eBay users, try contacting them before contacting eBay support. You may be able to guide them through the process if they're new buyers or determine that they have no intention of following through on the order.

- Open a case a few days after payment hasn't come through. The absolute latest is 32 days after the end of the auction or fixed price listing.

- If they have made a payment but it hasn't been electronically approved, wait an additional week before taking action.

Stock Seasonal Items

Whenever possible, take advantage of holidays and seasonal trends. Staying abreast of the season can make for a huge increase in sales for a temporary period of time. Take the time to add holiday greetings and seasonal tidbits to your packing slips and email correspondences. Embracing the current holiday is an easy way to draw in more buyers.

Study the Competition

One thing people fail to do when running an eBay business is taking the time to understand what their competition is doing with the same types of products. We suggested this before, but it deserves to be repeated. Taking the time to view other listings for the products you are trying to sell is how you can improve on their approach. If you read their listing and notice it doesn't include a detail you think it should, then it's obvious that you should include it. Likewise, if they list something you didn't think of and it impresses you, then take a leaf out of their book and do the same thing.

With an eBay store, this becomes especially important. Taking the time to study what has worked for other successful eBay entrepreneurs can teach you far more than shooting the breeze ever will. You don't want to be exactly like the competition, but you want to take the best of what they offer and then fill in the holes of what they don't offer as well to exceed them.

Be Friendly

While buyers can be picky, ask too many questions, and generally mean spirted or conniving at times, it is important to remember that old adage, "The customer is always right." This doesn't mean you have to bend over backwards to appease a scammer, but it does mean that you should be polite, always address people's issues with measures to resolve the problem, and be approachable in general. If someone asks a question, answer it thoroughly and without any snark. Being grumpy may just be your personality, but it doesn't translate well into sales or retaining great feedback scores.

Accept Returns

It may seem counter-intuitive starting out, as all returns come with a bit of loss in profits, but the truth of the matter is that it's difficult to avoid these anyway. If the buyer has a legitimate reason for a return, then eBay will allow them to open a case against you and force a return anyway. If the buyer doesn't have a legitimate case, they can just as easily try to open a case, and sometimes they may even win. It's truly less of a headache to just accept returns like most retail stores would. If you must, you can charge a restocking fee for those returns that aren't due to defects or other issues on your end.

If you take the time to write excellent descriptions, take excellent pictures, and ship your items properly, returns will be minimized. Make it a policy that you will accept returns for 30 days, but also make it a policy that the buyer must pay return shipping. If there's a defect of some type, you can do the right thing and pay for the return costs yourself anyway.

Write at an 8th Grade Level

One problem many educated people have is that they use big words. The truth is that many buyers may not be as educated, and the use of simple language tends to work better for sales, journalism, and just about anything other than poetry and fiction. Writing at an 8th grade level will be intelligent enough that nobody well educated will feel like you're insulting their intelligence, but it will also be simple enough that anyone without a great education won't feel like you're insulting their intelligence. Naturally, if you're selling items in a niche that relies heavily on jargon, you can still include this jargon in your listings.

Research Products Frequently

Stay on top of the trends! New products are coming out all the time, and your suppliers are likely adding new items to their inventory as well. Try to stay on top of new products as they are released, as a new product on the market is typically going to sell better before other sellers catch on to the sales and drive down the prices. New products are your chance for a boost in sales, and this can be a rather frequent event if you're truly taking the time to handle your product research on a frequent basis.

Avoid eBay Listing Add-ons

EBay offers a number of add-ons you can apply to your listings. This includes things like templates, bolded auction text, and highlighted auctions in search listings. These things don't do much to help you sell, and they just rack up the cost. Think about it. How often have you bought items that took advantage of these so-called promotional tools? Not very often I'd assume. About the only time it makes sense is with high-dollar items that are extremely rare and actually standout on their own anyway.

Don't Bother with Reserved Prices

Auctions with reserved prices are a waste of everyone's time. If you have a set price in mind, just list it as a fixed price and wait for the sale. People bidding on auctions are usually looking for a good deal. While a good bidding war may push it into retail pricing (sometimes above), the general bidder is going to bow out of a reserved auction and never be faced with the dilemma of how bad they want to win this item they've been watching and potentially bidding on all week. Reserved auctions do not help you make sales.

List Auctions on Sunday Afternoons

Sundays tend to be a high-traffic time because a large portion of the population have Sundays off. Auctions that end on Sunday afternoons will often see higher returns simply because the traffic on eBay is greater. For those on the east coast in the USA, listing between 6-9PM allows for west coast folk to also get in on the action. The more people that see the listing within the last few hours, the better your chances of selling your auctioned items at a higher price.

Use Auctions for Rare Items

For common items, there's really no reason to be using auction-style listings. Auctions are better for items that either don't have an obvious price point, or items that are so rare that they only come up once in a blue moon. If you have an item that is rare enough to demand a large sum of money, then take the time to promote this in communities that are likely to seek this item. For example, if you have a phonograph made in the 1940s and it's believed only a few hundred still exist in working order, then you need to scour the internet and social media for groups that collect these types of items, let them know you have it on eBay, and point them in the right direction. Maybe start a dialogue as well. They may be able to point you to folks that are willing to sell similar items.

Work Hard

While your goal is likely to leave behind a grueling job that doesn't pay well and forces you to be somewhere at a certain time every day, the truth about work is that it takes times and effort. Working hard is the only way you will succeed. Very few people have ever become financially stable by goofing off, and even when they did, there usually comes a time when their lack of initiative puts their business under.

Chapter 10: Promotion Techniques for Your eBay Business

While eBay is the largest marketplace and comes with a built-in customer base, that also draws in a lot of competition. Having a few promotional tricks up your sleeve will help people discover your store that may otherwise not run into it organically on eBay. We've talked about a few things regarding promotion, but there are some considerations that we haven't addressed fully. The knowledge you've learned thus far alongside this list should make it easy for you to piece together a marketing plan that works for the amount of time and money you can spare.

Seize Every Opportunity

Short of being extremely tacky, if there is an opportunity to mention your eBay store, then take the time to mention it. Telling people is the cheapest, easiest way you can possible promote yourself. A great example of this is adding a signature to your emails that links to your eBay account.

Include Advertisement in Packaging

When you ship an item, be sure to include some type of promotional material, whether it's just a thank you card with your logo or it's a full-fledged flyer with several of your commonly sold items on it, including some type of advertisement in your packages is a very inexpensive and simple way to remind the buyer about the seller who just gave them a good price, shipped quickly, and packaged their products safely.

Cross-promote Listings

At the end of your listings, you can either link to similar listings or remind buyers to take a moment to either see your other items for sale or visit your storefront. This is a great way to lure people into shopping from you alone. If you offer video games, there's a fairly good chance the person looking at one of your games may not buy it but would buy something else of yours after realizing you have fair pricing and a great reputation on eBay.

Share Listings Elsewhere

This applies largely to items that are either priced extremely well or are harder to come by. Rare items are great for sharing in other locations because people don't care if it's spam. If this incredibly difficult to find Bugs Bunny eraser is FINALLY on sale after not being on the market for years, some collectors are happy to hear through their usual forums and Facebook groups that you're going to be auctioning one off.

If you have a blog or a website, any pages that are relevant to link to one of your listings probably should link to one of your listings. If you create a high-quality blog with excellent content, the traffic generated from the blog can actually boost your business as well.

Use Multiple Categories

Some listings will allow you to choose two categories. While there may sometimes be fees involved, having your product in multiple categories makes it significantly more likely that potential buyers will land on your listing page and make a purchase.

Email Lists

Within your package adverts, website or blog, social media, and emails, you can ask your customers to join your mailing list. A mailing list is a powerful tool for staying connected with customers that are interested in the types of products you sell or the niche these products belong to. By having a mailing list that offers its own value, you can more easily encourage people to buy products from your eBay store as well. This works best for sellers within a specific niche rather than those that sell every product they can find.

Buzz Words for Titles

This applies both to listing titles and the name of your eBay store should you open one. EBay specifically suggests using these words because people often use them when searching. The list includes:

- New
- Unusual
- One-of-a-kind
- Estate sale

- Specialty
- Designer
- Unique
- Rare
- Powerful
- Vintage
- Collector's Item
- Inherited

Make sure the word actually applies to your listing. While having these buzz words may help with sales a bit, being dishonest is never the right method.

Attach a Domain Name to Your eBay Store

For those that have chosen the path of opening an actual eBay store and not just selling through listings alone, then it is wise to spend the $15 or so dollars per year for a domain name. If you run High Top Harry's Rare Rocks and Crystals, you might buy an address like "hightopcrystals.com," and simply have this redirected to your eBay store. This helps simplify the process of promotion, and it makes you look more professional as well.

There are quite a few places you can purchase a domain name. A few of our favorites are:

- http://godaddy.com
- http://google.com/domains
- http://namecheap.com

Craigslist and Social Media Buy Sell Trade Groups

It may seem a bit tacky to some people, but posting your eBay listings through Craigslist may not be a bad method of pushing a few more people towards it. The same can be said about Buy Sell Trade groups on Facebook, but take the time to make sure they allow this in their group, or you may just get banned. If people try to give you grief on Facebook for spamming, don't engage them. Getting a group of people that regularly buy online angry can lead to bad feedback from bored trolls.

High-Profile Auctions

This method isn't easy, but if you happen to find some Holy Grail type of item, it is possible to sell it on eBay, garner a ton of attention, and get a little bit of added business from it as well. Of course, you'll probably make a small fortune on this item too. There are many examples, one of the notable ones being the Nintendo Entertainment System game called "Stadium Events." There were only about 200 of these made in the United States, and this rarity and the rising interest in "retro" video games means that it has fetched as much as $35,000! Each time one appears on eBay, video game enthusiasts write hundreds of posts on their blogs, social media, and other outlets. This type of attention is great for an eBay seller, especially if it is leveraged to encourage people to check out your other, more reasonably-priced items.

Wrap It Up

There are so many perks to using eBay as your ecommerce platform that it's easy to see why so many people too off with the idea of opening an eBay store and were successful. They have created a selling platform with a huge built-in customer base, and they allow for auctions unlike any other online site can. It is such a remarkable force in the online market that it actually helps to set the retail value of items. It isn't perfect for every ecommerce goal, but it is quite sustainable as a business on its own.

EBay affords sellers to be less specialized than opening their own ecommerce store as well. While you should special within an eBay store setting, using it as an individual seller simply means providing great products at great prices and making sure the content is high enough quality that it is easily found through searches and explains the item and it's uses perfectly. It can also be used as part of a cross-platform sales method.

The true genius behind eBay is the simplicity of use. The user-friendly layout and design means that almost anyone can begin a career as an eBay seller. Through trial and error and continued research, the possibility of scaling an eBay business is very realistic through dropshipping. As your business grows, so does the knowledge that fuels your decision making. It requires some thinking and hard work, but it is so much more satisfying than working a "normal job."

Take the plunge. You can start your eBay business as a side gig while keeping your day job. At least take the time to get your toes wet. You wouldn't have read this book to this point if you weren't interested! Sell some of the items around your home you don't need, and decide for yourself if eBay is the opportunities you've been missing out on. You truly can change your life if you're willing to put in the hard work!